DATE DUE

BEAVERS

Based on the IMAX©/OMNIMAX© Motion Picture
A Stephen Low Film

SCHOLASTIC INC.

New York Toronto London Auckland Sydney

Based on the IMAX©/OMNIMAX© Motion Picture
BEAVERS
produced by Stephen Low Productions Inc.
for Chubu Electric Power Company Inc., Japan
©Dentsu Inc.

Filmed on location in Kananaskis Country,
Alberta, Canada

Director/Producer: Stephen Low
Executive Producer: Takashi Yodono
Director of Cinematography: Andrew Kitzanuk CSC
Underwater Photography: Stephen Low

All photographs from the film
©Dentsu Inc.

Text by Theresa Desmond

Library of Congress Cataloging-in-Publication Data

Desmond, Theresa.
Beavers / by Theresa Desmond;
photographs by Stephen Low/Picture Verse Productions.
p. cm.
"A Sue Katz & Associates, Inc. book"
ISBN 0-590-47084-1
1. Beavers—Juvenile literature. [1.Beavers.]
I. Low, Stephen, ill.   II. Title.
QL737.R632D475   1994
599.32'32—dc20
94-8512
CIP
AC

12 11 10 9 8 7 6 5 4 3 2 1   5 6 7 8 9/9 0/0

Printed in the U.S.A.

First printing, October 1995

Book design by Geoffrey Notkin and Jacqueline Ho
Illustration on pages 30–31 by Emma Crawford

This is the story
of how beavers make
their homes.

Deep in the Canadian woods, there is a wide, blue pond. A family of beavers lives in the pond. There is a mother and father, youngsters, grandparents, uncles, and aunts. The beavers made the pond themselves.

Many years ago, this land was rocky and wooded. Then one fall, two beavers made their way here. The shallow stream in the forest was the perfect place to make a home. Tall aspen trees grew beside the stream. Aspen leaves are one of the beavers' favorite foods. They also eat the bark of the tree.

The beavers make a dam and a shelter, called a lodge, from the branches and trunks of the aspen trees. An adult beaver can cut down more than 200 trees in one year.

Choosing trees close to the stream, the beaver stands on its back legs and grabs the tree with its small front feet. It turns its head sideways and begins biting and tearing at the trunk of the tree. Its big, orange-colored front teeth and strong jaws can pull off big chunks of wood.

The beaver works its way around the tree trunk until the trunk is almost chewed through. Then the tree comes crashing down. The beaver chews off the branches from the fallen tree. It grabs a branch with its front teeth and drags it to the water. If the tree is small, the beaver will drag the trunk to the water, too.

Now the beavers begin the slow, careful process of building the dam. They have already packed the bottom of the stream with mud and rocks. They pack the branches and tree trunks into the mud. Slowly, the dam begins to grow.

Many branches later, the dam holds firm. The stream is blocked off, and most of the water rises behind the dam. The water spreads over the small trees and bushes of the forest.

The dam is usually three or four feet high and can be more than 100 feet long. The beavers can make the pond bigger by adding more branches to the dam to make it higher. That makes the dam hold back more water.

The wide, quiet waters of the pond invite other animals in the forest to its shores. The pond becomes a home for fish, ducks, frogs, water bugs, and water snakes. Moose, deer, and foxes might come to the shore for a drink. Owls and other birds make homes in the tree stumps.

During the fall, the beavers build their lodge and gather food. They are preparing fo the cold winter. They will need shelter from the snow and cold air.

In the winter, beavers live in lodges. Some lodges are built into the banks of a river pond. Others are built in the middle of the pond. Lodges are built the same way as dams. The beavers pack branches into mud and rocks and make a domed island tha rises above the water.

The mud that holds the branches together freezes in the winter. It makes a shell that keeps the lodge dry and warm. Inside is a small chamber above the water level. The beavers make a soft bedding of shredded wood for the chamber floor.

They build water tunnels from the chamber to the bottom of the pond. During the fall, beavers store leafy branches in the mud at the bottom of the pond. Now, the beavers can swim beneath the ice to their food supply. They take the branches back to the lodge through the tunnels.

At the end of the winter, this female beaver gives birth to two baby beavers, called kits. The kits are born with fur and drink their mother's milk.

When spring comes, the ice on the pond melts. Then the beavers and kits emerge from the lodge. The kits swim, eat, play, and explore in and out of the pond. Their mother keeps a close eye on them. If she sees or senses danger, she slaps her flat tail on the water. The noise tells other beavers to head for the water.

Beavers' webbed back feet let them move more quickly in water than on land. A beaver can stay underwater for up to fifteen minutes on a single breath.

In the water, beavers are usually safe from their enemies. Their two most serious enemies are people and wolves. But sometimes an otter can swim into a lodge and attack the beavers. A hungry bear may even attack the lodge from the outside. And the small kits are in danger from hawks and owls, and even big fish.

In two years, some of the young beavers will leave the pond in search of mates. The older beavers force them to leave to make room for the newborn kits. The young beavers will try to find a place with flowing water and plenty of trees. Then they will build their own dam and lodge. The rest of the beaver family may stay in the same pond for many years.

But the dam might break. People or other intruders might tear it down. Severe weather might weaken the dam. If that happens, the pond water will run off and the stream will flow freely again. The land beneath the pond will dry up.

No other creatures, besides people, change the environment as much as beavers. What was once rocky forest land becomes a pond filled with wildlife. The forest is thinned out as the beavers cut more and more trees. If the dam breaks, grass and flowers will grow in the rich soil. The land will forever be different.

BEAVER LODGE, DAM, AND POND

1. Lodge

2. Dam

3. Underwater tunnel to lodge

4. Tree branches stored underwater

5. Old stream water level

6. New beaver pond water level

7. Tree stumps

8. Male beaver

9. Female beaver

10. Beaver kits (baby beavers)

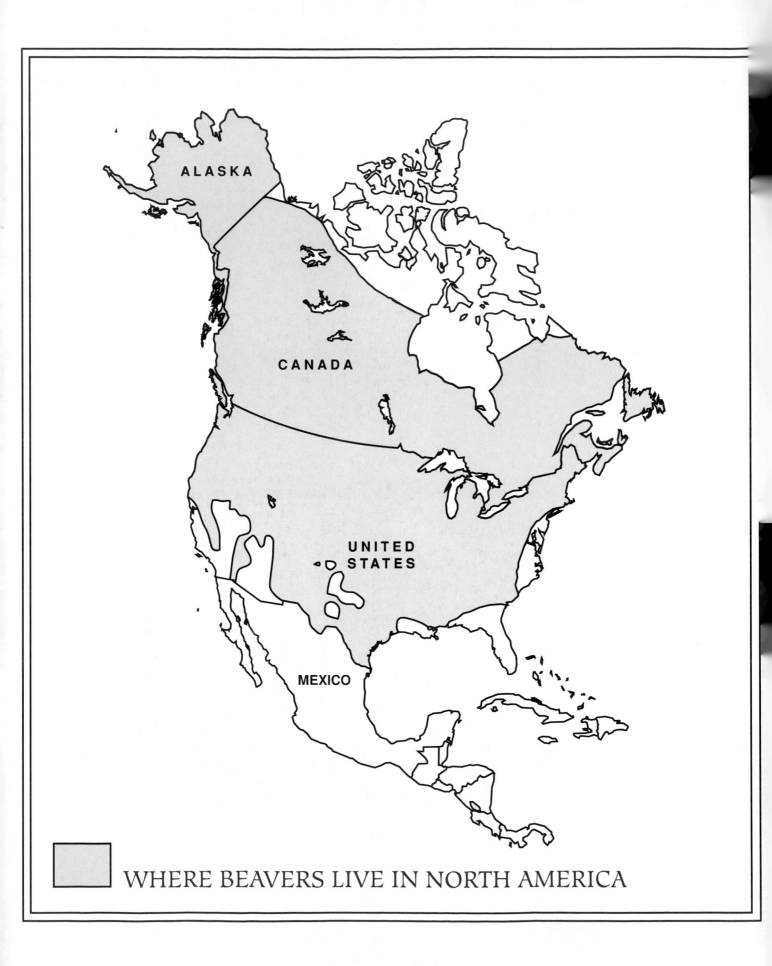

ALASKA

CANADA

UNITED
STATES

MEXICO

WHERE BEAVERS LIVE IN NORTH AMERICA